A Kid's Guide to Divorce and Life After It:

Tips, Tricks, and More

Daisy Freestone

Publishing support provided by
Ignite Press
5070 N. Sixth St. #189
Fresno, CA 93710
www.IgnitePress.us

ISBN: 979-8-9852203-0-8
ISBN: 979-8-9852203-1-5 (E-book)

For bulk purchase and for booking, contact:

DAISY FREESTONE
Book@DaisyFreestone.com

Library of Congress Control Number: 2021921599

Cover design by Swamynathan | 99Designs
Edited by Emma Hatcher | White Arrow Editorial Services
Interior design by Jetlaunch

FIRST EDITION

To Dad, whom I've always missed and wanted to spend more time with. I want to try to talk to you as much as I can and put in more of an effort to connect over the phone when I can't be there in person. I miss you more each day. I love you!

To Mom, who has always been there for me. Your support and love mean the world to me. You have put so much time, effort, energy, and money into helping me create this book and encouraging me to create freely and grow as a person. Thank you so much for everything you do! I love you!

Acknowledgements

This book could never have been possible without the friendly smiles and encouragement of these incredible people, so I would just like to give a big thank-you to them:

My mom, who has been so helpful and supportive and a great listener.

My many siblings, for putting up with me, making me laugh until I cried, entertaining me, and being so dang lovable and crazy all at the same time.

My dad, for working hard to connect with me, see me as much as possible, and make sure that I am comfortable and accommodated while at his house.

My stepmom, for spoiling me on shopping trips, geeking out over girly stuff with me, and keeping life interesting.

My stepdad, for giving me daily dad-joke doses, baking with me, and giving some of the warmest hugs in the universe.

My beautiful puppy, Bear, for giving me snuggles and licking my tears away when I'm sad.

My many aunts, uncles, and cousins, for hanging out with me, entertaining me, and doing awesome activities with me.

My Grandma and Grandpa Freestone, for taking me out to dinner, giving me fun toys, and being the sweetest, kindest grandparents ever (plus being AMAZING cooks).

My Grandpa Mathis, for making me laugh and showing me videos of Shirley Temple tap dancing as a little girl while we try to find shapes in popcorn.

And a big thanks to all of my readers and supporters!

Table of Contents

Mom's House Family

Introduction

Hi! My name is Daisy Freestone—fashionista, extreme nerd, bookworm, straight-A student, forever weirdo, and mastermind of *A Kid's Guide to Divorce and Life After It.* I was inspired to write this book because of the challenges that I face daily as a "divorce kid." If you're facing the same reality, I want to help you work through the difficulties of divorce, so you can be happy and free. I'll tell you a little bit about my story, and then we can dive right in!

I grew up happy and healthy; then, at the ripe age of five, it happened—my parents divorced. Things were actually okay for a while. It wasn't too shocking for me at first. My dad moved into an apartment close by, and I got to see him every other weekend and during the week too. It was like that for a long time, and I got used to it. I was happy, and I felt as if everything was perfect. Divorce is different for everyone, and maybe it was harder for you in the beginning. But for me, I was okay at the start. It was much more difficult down the road when new circumstances came. For example . . .

My dad started dating my now-stepmom long distance, and I mean LOOOOOOOONG distance. She lived in Missouri, and we lived in Texas. I didn't know it then, of course, but my whole life was about to change.

They dated for a while, and he went to visit her a lot. Eventually, he went on a beach vacation with her and her family and came back engaged! They married in 2017, and my dad decided to move in with her and my stepsisters. I was crushed. Devastated. Call it what you want, but you get the basic idea. It was really hard. I cried and fumed over it for weeks. Don't get me wrong, my new stepmom was really nice. But my dad leaving us? NOT exactly thrilling!

When everything started to feel okay again, of course, things had to change. My mom got a new boyfriend over the summer, and I met him at one point; so, I knew that things were getting serious. The good news though: he was a nice guy, and I could tell that he had good intentions. So, I did some matchmaking! You know, asking Bob if he had thought about marrying my mom, telling him she would make a great wife, yeah. I already had a stepmom; so, the idea of stepparents in general wasn't all that new to me. I figured that I could handle it.

Then we had a temporary move out of Texas halfway across the country. Yup.

I was so upset, even though it wasn't for forever. We began moving things out in boxes, and I just felt so helpless and overwhelmed and angry and sad and confused and irritated—all at the same time! I wanted my life to go back to what it had been before.

Moves and changes happen a lot after a divorce, and you don't have to like it. I certainly didn't! Maybe you can relate to what I'm saying, but if not, that's okay. Some people may even get excited about things like changes, even if other people don't like them at all. We are all different, and that's what makes us all so special. Anyway, back to the story . . .

Eventually, we got to the point where my room was SO empty that even the boxes were gone. It was just me, a roll of packing tape, and my bouncy ball with spikes on it. This is where I got to a point in my life where I felt the worst of any emotions that I ever could have felt. Every day before moving day, I sat on my spiky ball and faced an empty corner in my room. Then, I cried my heart out. Everything I felt poured out of me in a whirlwind of snot and tears; and I sat there for hours, crying until my throat was dry and my voice was gone. Most of my time was spent sulking.

I remember the first night in our new house—my mom and I lay down on a mattress in an empty room. We put our arms around each other and hugged, and I no longer felt numb. Everything came out. We both just cried and cried and cried until we couldn't cry anymore.

Over time, we started to settle into our new house and unpack everything. Bob drove all the way from Texas to visit us from time to time. He and my mom were doing great with long distance dating!

One time when he came to visit, he and my mom went on a hike in the morning. Long story short, he proposed to her. Soon after, they sat us—all of the kids—down at a restaurant to tell us. But unfortunately, the rest of my siblings were not doing so well with the transition. After a little bit of sarcasm and rude comments, we left the restaurant; even though not everyone was happy, everyone would get used to the idea of Bob becoming part of our family. He was a pretty cool guy, so that helped the process.

I started to have some things that I liked about Nevada. There was a huge, empty concrete lot by us, so we could scooter, bike, jump rope, and run all over the place there. Also, my aunt lived really close to us in our new house, and she introduced me to a girl my age.

I was pretty proud of myself for adjusting so well. Before I knew it, the school year was over, and we were moving back. WAIT, WHAT!?!? Yup. I had known it would be temporary, but still . . . more changes.

My mom was getting married, and we were heading back to Texas. I wasn't really that sad, or angry, or confused, but I kinda wanted to just say, "What the heck? I just got used to things here!" Also, I was having trouble staying in touch with my dad. We didn't talk enough, and I really missed him. This new big change was just one more thing that made everything hard, and I didn't have a lot of friends who could relate to that.

I was happy to be moving back to Texas in the same house that we had lived in before; but—as usual—change was coming! I had to go to a new school and, of course, get used to Texas again.

Over the last two to three years, things have settled down a little bit. I have a bunch of new friends at my new school, and I'm going to be in middle school next year. I used to have to share my room with two of my stepsisters, but now I have my own room and the two of them share a room. I go back and forth between Mom's house and Dad's house, my siblings come and go, me and my dad are trying to talk more, and by now I'm used to having ten siblings and four parents. I still miss my dad, and I still struggle with leaving his house, but I always have my mom to comfort me when I get home, and I always know that I'll go back to Dad's house at some point.

This is my story, and I know that our stories might be different. But I know that we can all relate to the big feelings that come from the changes in our lives. I hope this book helps you as much as possible. As you read, think about these experiences and ideas in a way that helps you the most. You're not alone. Thanks for reading!

Dad's House Family

Chapter 1

Intro to Divorce—What Is It?

What really is divorce and what does it mean? Divorce means that your parents have decided they don't want to be married anymore. Although your parents may not love each other anymore, it doesn't mean that they don't still love you. Your parents will always love you, no matter what their relationship is with each other.

Although your parents may not love each other anymore, it doesn't mean that they don't still love you.

Fantasies

When your parents first get divorced, you may be shocked. Or you might have seen it coming, but it can still be really hard. Your emotions can feel overwhelming and become a mess. Sometimes you just wish that your parents would get back together . . . AHA! That's it! You can formulate a brilliant plan to get your parents back together! Well, as easy as this might seem, it's probably *not* going to work. Remember, your parents had a reason for getting divorced. It could be messy. Your parents will most likely not get back together. Sometimes you might not be planning it out, just dreaming about it. Lots of kids do this, and it's *completely* normal. The problem is, even if you're just fantasizing, you may begin to think it will really happen. Always keep in mind that your life is NOT *The Parent Trap*. It's okay to dream about it once in a while, but you have to be careful and keep it real.

I bet they'll get back together!

New Circumstances

Divorce can cause many different circumstances, like maybe one of your parents will move out or you might have to move to a new house or even a new city, town, or state. If this happens, you might have to even give up a pet. It can be really sad, but you have to keep in mind that divorce is hard for everyone. Your parents might argue a lot and not get along. I have been very lucky because, in my experience, my parents get along and are friends. Not many kids are lucky like that; so, if you are, be grateful. And if you aren't, there are still good things about your situation.

It's not uncommon for parents to have bad feelings about each other after divorce and disagree all the time. If your parents keep fighting and arguing, you're not the only one. It happens to lots of kids all the time. Another thing that we're going to talk about that can be caused by fights between your parents is feeling stuck in the middle. You might hear one parent saying bad things about the other, or your parents will give you messages to tell the other parent. They might also ask you to pick sides in an argument, ask you who your favorite parent is, or ask for information about the other parent. These can all be uncomfortable, and it's important to let your parents know that you don't like it. If they say bad things about the other parent, you might want to say something like: "Mom/Dad, I don't like it when you say bad things about my other parent. If you're going to say things like that, please at least try not to when

I'm around. It makes me feel uncomfortable." If your parents want you to give messages to the other parent, ask them to tell the other parent themselves instead of involving you; and let them know that their trying to involve you makes you feel stuck in the middle. Those are just a few examples, but whatever the case, if you're feeling stuck in the middle, just let your parents know and ask them to stop. If it continues, just try to ignore it, or tell someone who can help you.

If you're feeling stuck in the middle, just let your parents know and ask them to stop.

Our last circumstance is emotion. Divorce can cause lots of high emotions for you or your siblings: sad, mad, confused, or scared. The emotions can even be happy, because some kids' parents argue a lot before divorce, and then the kids might want a break from it. If you need a break, try to find a way to relax as often as you need to. Go on a walk, talk to a friend, or write in a journal. Whatever works for you.

If you're having trouble coping with new circumstances, try working with your family, or maybe even friends, to come up with a solution or at least something that helps. You're not alone in this, and you can make it through as you build in some support.

Disconnection

Divorce sometimes causes disconnection between a kid and a parent, so it's important to try to spend time with, or talk to, both parents as much as possible after divorce. You or your parents might have a busy schedule, but even if you can just spare five to ten minutes to say hi on FaceTime, that's great. You will most likely feel really sad at first if one of your parents moves out, but you can just try to visit them as much as possible and try to talk to them a lot. Over time, you'll adjust to it and start to feel better. If you're really missing one parent or are not getting a lot of time with them, try talking to the parent you're living with and ask if there's a way to work out a schedule. For example, if you are missing your dad, you could ask your mom and see if maybe your dad could take you out for dinner on Wednesdays, and you could spend the day with him on Saturdays. Just make sure that it fits everyone's schedule and that everyone is happy with it.

Reasons and Blame

If you don't know why your parents are getting divorced, you should try asking them first. But chances are they will tell you, "grown-up reasons" or "We'll tell you when you're older." They may simply give you a vague answer that doesn't satisfy you or make sense. But it's important to remember that, whatever the cause of your parents' divorce may be, IT'S NOT YOUR FAULT. It never has been, and it never will be. Just because you were fighting with your siblings or you put up a fight about cleaning your room doesn't mean that you're the reason for the divorce. Of course, no parent likes it when kids do those things, but it has nothing to do with the divorce.

You are NOT to blame for your parents' decision. They have their reasons. You didn't do anything wrong. If you still don't believe me, ask your parents. They will tell you the same thing. It is 100 percent not your fault. Just try to make it easier for your parents, keeping in mind that they decided this on their own, not because of you.

But it's important to remember that, whatever the cause of your parents' divorce may be, IT'S NOT YOUR FAULT. It never has been, and it never will be.

You shouldn't just blame one of your parents either. Even if you feel like one of your parents simply walked out on the other, you never know what is really going on. It's important not to blame or judge one parent for the entire divorce. Parents get divorced for many reasons, and it's usually more complicated than being one person's fault or the other's. Your parents may not be getting along, they may be having financial issues, trust issues, or they might just not want to be married anymore.

Your Turn!

What circumstances have you gone through because of divorce? Which ones are especially hard for you? Is there one that you have already gone through or that you think you might go through in the future? What confuses you about divorce and how can you figure it out? What does your divorce situation look like?

No two situations are exactly the same, so I can't claim to understand what you're going through, because I may not. But whatever may be going on, with the help of your parents/friends/relatives, time, and a few books/workbooks like this one, you can figure it out and work through the challenges of divorce.

CHAPTER 2

Parents Dating/Marrying Again

AFTER YOUR PARENTS get divorced, they might start looking for someone to date. They might even get remarried. This chapter will guide you through the possibility of one or both of your parents dating and marrying again, so you can have a happy, healthy relationship with your parents and whoever they're dating/married to.

Parents Beginning to Date Again

When your parents first start dating again, it can definitely feel weird, especially when a parent introduces you to their new boyfriend/girlfriend. It will probably feel strange to see your parent with someone else other than your mom/dad. Or maybe your parents have been divorced for a while and you're used to seeing your parent alone. Whatever the case, it's going to seem odd at first.

You might feel angry at your parent for being with someone else or feel angry at your parent's boyfriend/girlfriend for "stealing" your parent. Or you might feel confused if you actually like someone your parent is dating and think that they're really nice or funny, etc. Whatever you're feeling, you should talk to your parent so that they can help you.

Even if you don't like your parent's boyfriend/girlfriend, you need to be polite. Don't be rude to them; and, if they start a conversation with you, you need to respond to them and keep an open mind. Who knows, they might be really nice once you get to know them. Even if you don't really like them once you get to know them, focus on the good about them. You need to at least find ONE thing you like about them, because if things go well between them and your parent, you might have to live with them.

> You need to at least find ONE thing you like about them.

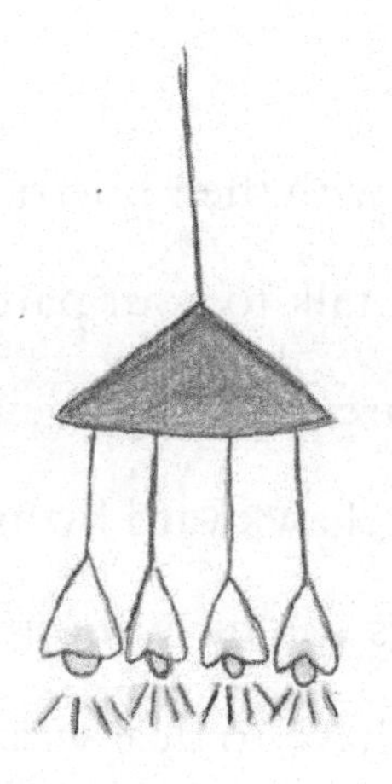

Family game night!
And we ordered a pizza!

Serious Dating and Engagement

If you can tell that your parent is getting serious with their boyfriend/girlfriend and it's making you uncomfortable, you should talk to your parent and see if you can spend time with friends while your parent is with their new significant other. This might help so that you don't feel awkward by having to be in that situation. If the ideas to change the feelings you have about your parent's relationship aren't working out, you might just have to deal with it.

If your parent and parent's significant other tells you that they're engaged, your initial reaction will probably be something like "WHAAAAAAT?!?!?" If you're lucky, you'll have gotten used to the dating thing. But even if you have, the news will still probably come as a big shock. They might even ask you to be in the wedding. And, if you don't like your new stepparent, chances are, you won't want to. But think of it as a favor for your parent. If you've really thought about it and you still decide not to, decline politely and still attend.

You might not get what I'm saying. Or your situation might be like mine: Your parent ends up dating someone you really like. When my mom told me that she was engaged to Bob (her boyfriend at the time and a person I really liked), I was ecstatic. I had actually (believe it or not) asked Bob to consider marrying my mom, because I saw that he was a really nice guy who genuinely loved my mom for who she was. She was happier with him, and I wanted her to be happy. Anyway, they asked me to be a flower girl in the wedding, and I gladly agreed. It was a great, fun experience. Bob and my mom are still a perfect match and happy couple to this day. I'm glad that I gave Bob a chance, because he's a great guy.

How to Prepare

When your parents are about to get married, you should probably find a way to prepare for having a stepparent. They might move in with you, and that can be hard. You need to find something that you have in common with them or something that you can bond over. Say, for example, you like football, and your soon-to-be stepparent does too. Even if you don't like the same teams, you can still watch football together and talk about the game.

If you think that you'll get upset or lash out often after you get a stepparent, take some time to yourself and relax the week before the wedding or the day before the wedding. Just prepare yourself to stay calm, cool, and collected.

Your Turn!

What do you think about your parents dating or getting married again? If this is happening or has already happened, what has been hard for you about it? What positive things can you take from your parents dating and/or marrying again?

No matter if you like your parent's spouse-to-be or not, there's a marriage coming up, and you need to prepare—because you're about to get a stepparent, and with that often comes a whole new "family."

Chapter 3

Figuring Out Stepfamily

Once your mom or dad has gotten remarried, you've entered the world of stepfamily. There's going to be lots of changes to get used to, so get ready.

Stepsiblings

Your stepsiblings might be reluctant to open up to you at first, but hopefully they'll eventually warm up to you. It might take a while, or they may never warm up; but if or when they do, you will probably become best friends. You will probably also fight a lot, but that's completely normal. It can be really fun to have stepsiblings, because it can give you another person (or a few more people) to play with. The only problem is, it might not be as much fun if they aren't around your age. You might start to get jealous if it feels like your parent gives them a lot of attention. You might not like sharing a room (if you have to) or other living spaces with them, but it's important to keep an open mind. If you're having trouble getting along, I suggest that you all sit down and talk about why you're upset.

Stepparents

Stepparents are kind of the opposite of stepsiblings. They'll usually try to be in your life and engage with you right away. While it's important to know that they will never take your original mom/dad's place, they are still your family and deserve your love and respect. Like stepsiblings, they can be fun to spend time with. Also, they can be like stepsiblings in other ways, because, like I said earlier, you may become jealous of them. Maybe even more so than stepsiblings, because your parents are in love with them. But just remember that your parents love you just as much as ever and will always have a special place in their heart for you that no one can take away. Make sure that you have time to connect with your stepparents too!

> Just remember that your parents love you just as much as ever and will always have a special place in their heart for you that no one can take away.

Ideas

Is it betraying Dad to like Mom's house better?
Should I feel BAD that I miss Dad so much?
LONELY
CONFUSED
ANGRY
SCARED

I have a lot of experience with divorce and stepfamily, but that doesn't mean it's become a perfect life for me. I still fight with my stepsiblings and stepparents a lot, like when my stepsisters come over. Me and one of my stepsisters start fighting, and then the other one gets upset that we're fighting and they both leave. Or sometimes we get into a three-way argument, and we all get really frustrated. What really helps is to take a break from each other and, once you've all calmed down, sit together and talk about what frustrated each of you and how to fix it. Another thing that has happened is when my stepdad will give me a job and I get mad and say things like "You're not my real parent! You can't tell me what to do!" Then we get in a fight and I run upstairs. When you get in a fight with a stepparent, you should try to work it out yourself. If you can't, have your biological parent help you sort it out.

Your Turn!

What experience do you have with stepfamily? Have you ever gotten into a fight with them? If so, how did you fix it? What ideas can you try in the future?

Stepfamily can take a little while to adjust to, but hopefully you can figure it out and get used to it. It's important to have a friend or someone else to talk to if you're having issues with your stepfamily, so have a person or two to help you.

CHAPTER 4

Blending Families

BLENDING FAMILIES CAN be tough. Things may not fall into place and blend very easily at all. Your new "family" might not accept you right away, or maybe you might not accept them at first. It's normal, because a lot of kids just want their family to stay the same as they were before.

Getting Used to It and Getting to Know Each Other

Big changes are hard, and it may be too much to just jump in and try to be a family right away. Try starting out by simply getting to know your stepsiblings/stepparents/half-siblings, and then take it from there.

Speaking of half-siblings, that might be a difficult change too. It can DEFINITELY feel like your parent gives them more attention, especially if they're just a baby. If this happens to you, try to remember that they are now your parent's kid, too, and that they deserve love and attention as much as you do. And again, it might not feel like family right away, but hopefully it will one day. Do your best to make them feel welcomed and loved. If your half-sibling doesn't live with you, try to stay connected with them as much as possible.

As you're getting to know your new "family," I suggest trying to find things you have in common. It may help so that you have something to talk about and maybe even bond over. If it seems like there's nothing to talk about, remember that you all have one thing in common: you've experienced divorce. If it's a sensitive or awkward subject for them and they don't want to talk about it, don't push it. Just try and find something else to talk about. Remember that you've also got people in your family in common and you're all trying to figure out how to blend families. Some of the big challenges of divorce can be common ground for all of you.

Also, in blended families, it can sometimes feel chaotic or crazy. If you need a break, just try to find a quiet, calm place. If you can't find one in the house, maybe you can go outside and find one. And if the other kids in your new family are missing one of their parents, try and help them. You're going through the same thing. Try and find something to cheer them up, and maybe someday they'll return the favor! One time, one of my stepsisters got really sad and missed her mom a lot. She started crying, and my other stepsister and I rushed to comfort her. I told her, "It's going to be okay. Think of the fun things you'll do with her when you get home and make a list. When you see her again, you can do all of it together." She thought about it, and it helped her relax. A few days later, I was missing my dad, and she helped me by telling me the same thing. When you have each other, it really helps you get through hard things.

When you have each other, it really helps you get through hard things.

Sharing Spaces, Complications, and Boundaries

There's definitely going to be a lot of things that are different to adjust to. It can be really difficult to get used to these big changes. It feels complicated having a big family, and sometimes you wish that things would go back to "normal." For example, I live with my mom and my stepdad (in my mom's house). When my stepsisters come over, sometimes I feel jealous, because they get to be with their dad and it makes me really miss my dad. Then I start missing my other stepsiblings from my dad's side, and my stepmom, etc.

Another thing when they come over is that sometimes they make me feel left out, because they whisper to each other and tell secrets without me all the time. You have to learn to get along well, and if you have to share a room or other space . . . ughhhhh. It can make you feel possessive of the space, because you're used to it being just yours. It can also feel cramped and/or crowded, and you might feel like there's not enough room. You should talk to your parent/stepparent and see if there's a different way to divide up spaces or just talk to whoever you're sharing the room with and split the space in halves, etc.

You also need to make sure that there's boundaries on things. If there's something you and your "siblings" are going to share, make sure it's available to all of you and not just hogged or taken by one person. But if there's something that's special or specifically belongs to just one person, make sure your "siblings" know and have rules on it, like "You can only use it if you have asked first," or "Please don't touch it, but you can look at it, and I can show you how to use it," or something similar. Having some rules and boundaries helps make it easier to agree, work things out, and get along.

Having some rules and boundaries helps make it easier to agree, work things out, and get along.

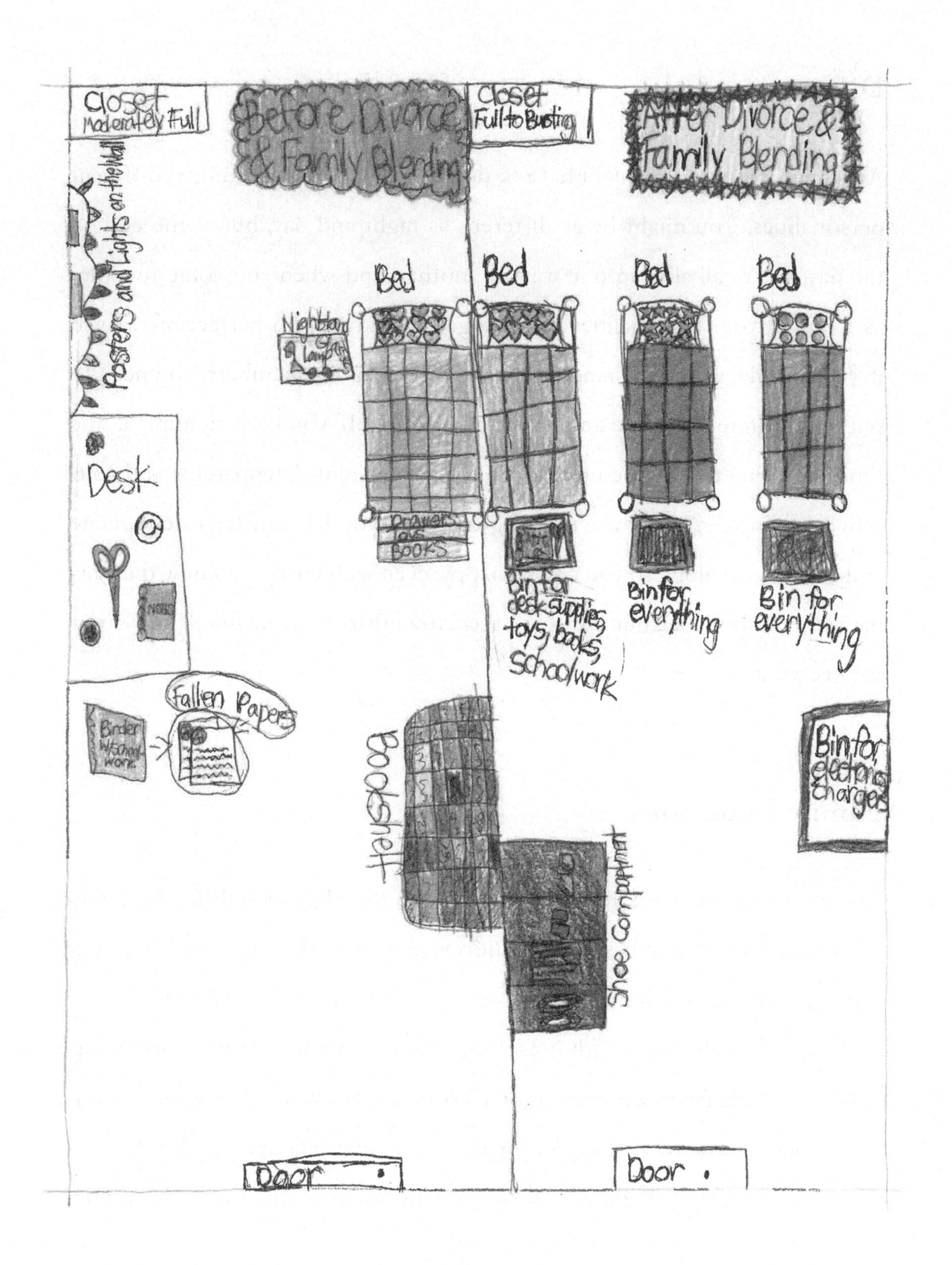
Closet Moderately Full
Before Divorce & Family Blending
Closet Full to Busting
After Divorce & Family Blending
Posters and Lights on the Wall
Bed
Bed
Bed
Bed
Nightstand Lamp
Drawers Toys BOOKS
Desk
Bin for desk supplies, toys, books, schoolwork
Bin for everything
Bin for everything
Fallen Papers
Binder w/schoolwork
Bookshelf
Bin for electronics chargers
Shoe Compartment
Door
Door

Differences

Another thing that you might have to deal with in a blended family is different personalities. You might be as different as night and day, but at the end of the day, you're all alike in one way or another, and when you come together as a family, your personalities blend together and make a perfect mix. Even if you feel like you can't stand one of your new family members, you need to put your differences aside and learn to get along. If you keep fighting all the time, it's going to become unbearable for your parents/stepparents and your other "siblings." And if you're living together, you have to try to cooperate and learn to get along so you can be happy, even with change. I know that this may seem impossible, but it's worth the extra effort to make life a little easier for everyone.

Family Traditions

The last thing that we're going to talk about in this chapter is different family traditions. Not all families have traditions, but most do. You might be of a different religion or ethnicity than some of your new family members, and so, you might have different traditions. It doesn't have to be a tradition related to that though. My family eats nachos on Christmas Eve just because we like them. That's one of our traditions. As for religion, some religions don't celebrate the same holidays that you do. Or they might just celebrate them differently.

I celebrate Christmas, but Jewish people don't. Some people don't have a religion. Not everyone does. And that's perfectly okay. We don't all believe in and celebrate the same things. And when you get a new family, you'll have to learn to blend traditions. As I said before, my family has a tradition of eating nachos for Christmas Eve dinner, but my stepdad and his biological kids have a tradition of eating fondue on Christmas Eve. We have had to find a way to compromise or combine the two. For example, switching off each year or putting the fondue meat and cheese on the nachos! If you have conflicting traditions as well- try to get creative. You could even pick a new tradition altogether as you blend families.

If your new family isn't all one religion or ethnicity, you should try new and different things, like celebrating Hanukkah for the first time with your new family if they celebrate it. If you don't agree with their religion or culture's beliefs, you can still be polite. You don't necessarily have to celebrate their holidays or participate in their traditions in order to love and accept each other.

Your Turn!

What does your blended family look like? What things have been hard for you in blending families? What things have been easy? How can you resolve issues in your blended family and enjoy time together?

Blending families is hard, but once you get the hang of things and learn to talk to your family members to work out any issues, you'll have it figured out and you can enjoy time with your new family.

CHAPTER 5

The Good Things No One Tells You About Divorce

DIVORCE, PARENTS DATING again/remarrying, and blending families are all challenges, and they can be hard to face. But as difficult as divorce can be, there can also be some good things about it that no one told you.

But as difficult as divorce can be, there can also be some good things about it that no one told you.

Learning from Divorce

You'll learn a lot by going through divorce, and you'll become more mature. Divorce teaches you many things!

Here are just a few of the things that you'll have an opportunity to learn:

- How to get along with others

  With stepsiblings, half-siblings, or stepparents, you'll have to try lots of different techniques for getting along with others, cooperating, and working as a team. If you get in fights with your new family, you'll need to figure out how to resolve whatever issues you're having. And being family, at some point, you'll probably endure some crazy situations together, so you'll learn teamwork and creativity in the process.

- How to face challenges

  As I just said, you'll probably endure some crazy situations in the world of divorce. You'll learn how to face and embrace challenges and hard things. You'll need it in life, because when difficulties arise, you need to be able to work with them.

- Bravery

  You need to be able to deal with scary things and stand strong. Even if you're terrified, you need to gather your courage and keep going. Divorce teaches you bravery, because it gives you situations that you don't want to deal with and are afraid to deal with. After a little while as a "divorce kid," you learn more ways to be brave and keep moving.

- How to go with the flow

Nobody really asked you if you wanted your parents to get divorced or if you wanted a different family. Divorce will teach you that you don't always get what you want and that not everything is up to you. You just have to go along with / find the bright sides for whatever happens.

- Empathy

Divorce is a hard situation to deal with, and it's not always easy, especially if you have other things to deal with that you're not used to, like several new family members or sharing a room. Divorce will teach you empathy and how to be sympathetic for others who are dealing with hard things. When you have experience with something really difficult, it will be easier to feel sympathetic for someone else going through something challenging.

- How to deal with family issues

This kind of relates to getting along with others. If there's family drama or a fight, you'll learn how to deal with it. So, in the future, when family issues/problems come up, you can deal with them appropriately.

Before Divorce
hair hanging in eyes
slouching
hoodie
Shy
Nervous
Quiet
After Divorce
Brave
new haircut
hopeful
no hoodie
shoulders risen
happy
Confident
Outspoken
Resilient

Bonus Things from Divorce

If you celebrate Christmas, you might do it at two or even more houses now because of divorce. And you know what that means . . . DOUBLE PRESENTS!! Even if one of your parents lives really far away, they can still send you presents in the mail. My dad lives in another state, and my parents switch off for holidays. So, one year my mom has me for Christmas, and the next year, my dad does. What we do is if I have Christmas at my dad's house, my mom does "early Christmas" with me and my brothers before we leave. And if I have it at my mom's house, my dad just sends me gifts in the mail. See? DOUBLE PRESENTS!! The same thing goes for birthdays. I always have my birthday at my mom's house, but sometimes my dad comes to visit for it. If he can't, he'll send me gifts in the mail. Even if one of your parents doesn't really visit or communicate with you, there's still a lot of great things that you can take from divorce. Another bonus that you might get is more people in your life, which can mean more love, more quality time with those you love, more siblings to play with, and more fun experiences. In other words, as confusing, annoying, and crazy as a big or new family can be, it can still be a lot of fun. Or you might get to spend more time with just one of your parents, which helps you stay connected. The last bonus that I want to talk about is that your parents may be a lot happier after the divorce. They might still love your other parent and be sad, but they might also be happy about the divorce and feel better. Your parents probably weren't very happy fighting, so it can feel good to have constant conflict be over for them.

New Experiences from Divorce

Another good thing about divorce is that you might get to have new experiences. For example, if you have never been to a Chinese restaurant but one of your new family members loves it, you might go there for lunch someday and find out that you like it. Or, if you are used to sitting around and watching television all weekend but your stepsiblings like going to a dance class and want you to join, you might go and fall in love with dance. A new experience could even have something to do with family, like if you became the middle child for the first time. It could even be a new experience having siblings. Maybe you were an only child before. Whatever the case, divorce brings new experiences that you might not have had otherwise.

Your Turn!

What are good things that you have experienced because of divorce? What are some other good things that you might get to experience in the future? What are your favorite things about your life now?

Divorce has its challenges, but there can be good things about it to look forward to and enjoy. Few people will tell you about these, so you might think that divorce is only bad. But there can be some great things about it, even if it's not always fun.

Chapter 6

Getting Over It

Once you've mostly figured out all of the aspects of divorce, there's still one part left: really *getting over it* fully. You might be happy and think that you have it all figured it out; and you might. But if you really think about it, do you still feel a little empty?

The truth is that you might never fully get over it. I've been a divorce kid since I was four or five, and I still feel really sad about it sometimes. I miss my dad all the time, and I get confused in my big family now and then. Your life will never be truly perfect, and that's okay. Really, there is no such thing as perfect anyway. Even kids who aren't in a divorce situation have challenges. You might adjust and be fine, but if it's still a challenge for you, don't be discouraged. Divorce being a challenge is really normal, and you're not alone. I promise that there is hope!

Acceptance
SADNESS
ANGER
FEAR
denial
SHOCK
DIVORCE

If you feel fine with your situation and feel like you're okay, you can go. You're done here. Congratulations! But if you ever feel the need to crack this book open again, go ahead. You might get over the divorce for a while and then start struggling again. When I was younger, I was really sad, and I didn't get what was going on at all. Then I got a little older and accepted divorce. I felt fine with my situation, and I was happy. Then I got older again, and it became hard and sad again. It really changes, and any way that you feel about it is perfectly fine. You may never completely get over it, and that's alright. But you can try to enjoy how your life is right now.

With divorce, there's a lot of things that you'll miss. Parents, pets, simplicity . . . you just have to learn to cope. It's really hard to deal with sometimes, and emotions can be overwhelming. Try different solutions and see what works for you. Remember, humans have emotions. It's okay to feel sad, angry, or upset. Divorce isn't easy, and when it comes to coping, you just have to work it out. The solutions that I use might not work for you, or your solutions might not work for others. That's okay. Everyone is different.

It's okay to feel sad, angry, or upset.

Your Turn!

What strategies do you have to cope? What do you do when your emotions feel overwhelming? What are the best things about your new life?

Divorce is a big thing, and it's difficult to get over and cope with. You should feel proud of yourself for working hard to move forward. Give yourself a pat on the back! You're stronger than you realize, and I hope you remember that. I hope that this book has helped you to its full ability and that, while your life will never be "picture perfect," you can get used to divorce and love your life. Even if things didn't line up the way that you wanted them to or the way you thought they should, your life is still amazing and has some great aspects that you'll come to love and appreciate.

Review Inquiry

Hey, it's Daisy here.

I hope that you've enjoyed the book as much as I loved writing it! I have a favor to ask you.

Would you consider giving it a rating wherever you bought the book? Online bookstores are more likely to promote a book when they feel good about its content, and reader reviews are a great reflection of a book's quality.

So, please go to the website of wherever you bought the book, search for my name and the book title, and leave a review. If able, perhaps consider adding a picture of you holding the book. That increases the likelihood your review will be accepted!

Many thanks in advance,

Daisy Freestone

Will You Share the Love?

Get this book for a friend, associate, or family member!

If you have found this book valuable and know others who would find it useful, consider buying them a copy as a gift. Special bulk discounts are available if you would like your whole team or organization to benefit from reading this. Just contact Book@DaisyFreestone.com.

Would You Like Daisy to Speak to Your Organization?

Book Daisy Freestone now!

Daisy accepts a limited number of speaking engagements each year. To learn how you can bring her message to your organization, email Book@DaisyFreestone.com.

About the Author

I LIVE IN Frisco, Texas, with my mom, my stepdad, my puppy (named Bear), and my two older brothers. I am eleven years old, and I have ten siblings, ages two, nine, nine, eleven, thirteen, sixteen, seventeen, eighteen, nineteen, and twenty. I love reading, swimming, soccer, dancing, singing, baking, fashion, and hairstyling. My favorite color is green. My favorite food is a burger and fries. My favorite music genre is pop, my favorite book genre is realistic fiction, my favorite television show is *High School Musical: The Musical: The Series*, and my favorite movie is *Z-O-M-B-I-E-S*.

Daisy can be reached at: www.DaisyFreestone.com.

Made in the USA
Las Vegas, NV
13 December 2024